ARTISTS OF THE

AMERICAN WEST

CONTENTS

Published by
CASTLE BOOKS
A Division of
BOOK SALES, INC.
110 Enterprise Avenue
Secaucus, New Jersey 07094

INTRODUCTION

The American "West" of the 1820s became the American "Far West" of the 1850s. That, in turn, became the American "Wild West" ever after. It has given us many unique legends and historical subjects: cowboys, Indians, charging cavalry, ghost towns, mountain men, and "The Wide Open Spaces." These are all part of what makes Western art unique in not only America's but also the world's history.

Western art is one of the few "schools" of art that is defined by a selection of subjects rather than a technique. Impressionism could refer to anything painted as the feeling of the artist rather than the exact duplication of the object he was painting. But Western art, which was occasionally "Impressionist," was defined by its subject matter. It had a specific purpose: to record and comment on the events, inhabitants, and characteristics of America's Western states.

For that reason, Western art, unlike other forms of media, did not have a profound influence overseas. While Europeans like the German Karl May wrote droves of stories about cowboys, Indians, and gunfighters, and Western songs became music-hall favorites, painting of Western subjects was still limited to work done by Americans in America. It seemed that the rest of the world felt that the rendition of such detail should be left to those who were there to witness the West at first hand.

But if Western art is so specifically defined, it must seem strange that the artists who practiced it were not grouped together in stylistic schools. These artists were independent people, and rather than cooperate, they often developed intense rivalries. Remington and Schreyvogel painted in amazingly similar styles, yet Remington criticized the works of Schreyvogel, setting off a nationwide debate. Some of these artists, such as Farny, who studied under the group of "Ten" in New York, dramatically turned away from all recognizable schools, simply to be free of their influence. They were truly "rugged individualists."

Much of the work of the earlier artists of the West was financed and encouraged by the United States government and American business. Seth Eastman, for example, was an official illustrator for the Department of Indian Affairs in Washington. Other artists, such as Catlin, Stanley, Bierstadt, Moran, and Miller, accompanied official exploring expeditions. Their illustrations of the new frontier played a significant role in the course of American history. Not only did these works encourage settlers to move out West; Moran's representation of what is now Yellowstone encouraged Congress to create the national parks system.

After the Civil War, the new mass media, particularly magazines, began to hire artists to create dramatic illustration for their editions. Several careers were started and maintained by *Harper's Weekly* alone, and *Scribner's* and *Outing* were not far behind in such sponsorship. The development of illustration contributed mightily to a change in the nature of Western art. The need of the Eastern media for exciting accounts and drawings of the West caused Western art to become increasingly mythical and less realistic in style.

By the 1850s, a new trend was developing: Romanticism. Carried back from Europe, this emotional idealization of what the artist saw transformed Western horizons into gigantic plains and misty mountains. Bierstadt's enormous canvases thrilled the Easterners with their expansive view of a nature so large that even Victorian technology, the technology of the railway era, could not hope to subdue it. The wild dramas and nostalgic yearnings in the paintings of Bierstadt and other Romantics fueled a new drive by both the poor and the intellectual to live in such a splendid land.

After the Civil War, however, America entered a new period. Progress became the slogan of the times and the excuse for a profound social upheaval. The art of the West, tied to its subjects, was suddenly engulfed in protracted warfare between Indians and settlers, Indians and Cavalry, settlers and outlaws, miners and ranchers. For almost fifty years the West was wracked by massive, organized violence. The Indian Wars, which ultimately crippled and eviscerated the Indian cultures, became the vortex for such later artists as Remington and Schreyvogel. Others, like Russell, shunning the violence, turned to the activities of daily life that had to continue amidst the turmoil. As the resistance of Indian leaders such as Geronimo, Cochise, and Sitting Bull—and the military campaigns of cavalry leaders like George Custer—became the stuff of legend, artists like Farny, Johnson, and Wyeth developed strong mythologies. The era of realism was long gone, and by the 1860s Romanticism, too, was giving way. Legends had taken over the consciousness of the West, and mythology was king.

The art of the West, up to this time, had been a unique phenomenon. Such early artists as Catlin and Bierstadt were popular as well as critical successes. There was no difference in Western art between popular and classical forms. However, by the turn of the century, Western art had succumbed to the rapidly developing differences between academic and mass culture in America. Wyeth, Johnson, and Farny represented the new popular Western ideal. But others, such as Georgia O'Keeffe and Thomas Hart Benton, verged to the classical: an art using Western subjects but which was now more concerned with technique than with preservation or mythification of the Indian, the land, or the cowboy.

Once, Western art had helped to draw people from the East to the purity and splendor of the lands of the American West. But in doing so, it also encouraged the encroachment of technology, engineering, and the worst of Eastern civilization. By encouraging settlement, Western art had also encouraged wars that resulted in the decimation of the Indians it had so highly praised, and the end of the unfenced openness so unique to the plains. This wonderful form of art, so fresh and so alive, so unbounded by schools and national traditions, had done exactly what it had not wished to do: it had ultimately assisted in the destruction of the area it so fervently wished to preserve. Today, it stands as a memorial to something youthful, spontaneous, and unlimited in the heart of America.

GEORGE CATLIN

The fascination of George Catlin (1796–1872) with the Indian was one of the key factors in the development of Western art. His work was so influential that after Catlin, artists flocked to the West in search of the exotic native cultures that were fast being destroyed by the white man's relentless expansion. As a child Catlin's mother had been briefly kidnapped by Indians, and the boy himself bore a long facial scar from an accidental tomahawk blow. Born in Wilkes-Barre, Pennsylvania, Catlin was given a solid formal education that eventually led to a law degree, but he longed to pursue his study of Indian cultures. In 1821, he began to paint, and gave up his law practice. After moving to Philadelphia he turned his attention fully to art, and by 1824 had achieved such renown that he was elected to the Pennsylvania Academy. There, he met a group of visiting Indians, and their effect on him was so electric that he determined to paint all the tribes in North America. From that point on, Catlin travelled the width of America recording what he felt were the last examples of the unchanged American native. He joined an expedition headed by William Clark (of the Lewis and Clark journeys) that led him to Kansas and Missouri in 1830. In 1832, after a trip up the Yellowstone, he published an anthropological tract, *Letters and Notes on the Manners, Customs, and Conditions of the North American Indians*; it was one of the first works of its kind, and was written in great scope and detail. Between 1833 and 1837, he travelled further west than any previous artist had ventured, down lengths of the Missouri, Red, and Blue Rivers, recording everything from buffalo hunts and sham battles to strange rites of initiation. Then, in 1837, Catlin ended his western travels and collected his works in a vast show, which he named The Indian Gallery. His success was both immediate and enormous. Not only did he display these works in New York and Washington––they were also printed as lithographs and shown to great acclaim in Europe. His one great disappointment was in failing to convince the United States government to buy his Indian Gallery for the public. Catlin worked with an almost unbelievable energy; in 1832 alone, he produced over 135 paintings. Many of these were hastily sketched and only later completed, and the details are therefore not always accurate. For this reason, his reputation has suffered many assaults. However, his vigor and freshness have kept him in the forefront of artists who chronicled the final years of Indian independence.

Buffalo Chase in Winter, Indians on Snowshoes (1832)
This painting indicates both the strengths and flaws of Catlin's work: On the one hand, the depiction of the fleeing lines of buffalo is unnaturalistically clean and orderly; moreover, few Indian buffalo hunts were executed by riding parallel to the running herds—normally, the Indians crept up on the herds, surrounded them, and converged. On the other hand, the depiction of the running action is carried out with Catlin's eye for minute detail and vivid coloration, encouraging the viewer to feel the excitement of speed and effort experienced by both prey and predator.

ALFRED JACOB MILLER

Alfred Jacob Miller (1810–1874) was the first of the artists of the American West to sketch the fur traders and Indians of the Rocky Mountains, and was, in fact, the first of his profession to travel as far west as the Wyoming Territory. Unlike Catlin, Miller studied extensively in Europe, particularly in Paris and Rome, and he was heavily influenced by the Romantic movement of the mid-1830s. Although born in Baltimore and trained by Thomas Sully, his life as an artist did not achieve significance in America until he joined the expedition of the Scotsman W.D. Stewart. The expedition left Missouri in early 1837, and after passing such outposts as Fort William (later, Fort Laramie), passed on into the Rocky Mountains themselves, where Miller sketched mountain men and such Indian tribes as the Shoshone, who had never before been recorded. Miller was particularly fascinated by the friendly relations between the trappers and their Indian allies, and his field sketches helped later historians to understand the complex interactions of the white man and the Indian in those early days when the fur trade was making such a tremendous impact on the drive to open the West. In 1840 Captain Stewart inherited a title and a castle in Scotland, and Miller followed him there to complete full oil paintings from the watercolor sketches he had made during the expedition. He remained for two years, after which he returned to Baltimore, where he lived a comfortable but sedate existence until his death in 1874. Miller served as a bridge between the early anthropologists and the later Romantics, combining a fascination with his subject matter and a strong emotional quality. His paintings are often moody and nostalgic, but represent places, people, and events with a sense of normal scale. His works capture a harmonious quality between white men and Indians that was soon to disappear in the blood and turmoil of the Civil War and the Indian Wars of the later part of the century.

Shoshone Indian and Pet Pony (1837)
This oil is derived from sketches made during the Stewart expedition in 1838, and, as such, it is full of the romantic nostalgia that permeated Miller's later works. The detailed rendering of the Indian, his white horse, and the teepee in the background contrast vividly with the cavernlike mystery of the tent's interior and the distant expanse of plain to the left. The horse is the key element in the painting, its vigorous shape contrasting strongly with the placid figure of the Indian seated behind him. What the painting may lack in clinical realism is compensated for by its evocative mood and a certain quiet spiritualism.

GEORGE CALEB BINGHAM

George Caleb Bingham (1811–1879) was an artist favored by fortune in almost every way. Once he began to paint, he never lacked material comfort or personal recognition. His successful career included many political interludes, and by the end of his life he had achieved the rank of full professor of art. Bingham was born to modest circumstances in Virginia, and moved to Franklin, Missouri when he was eight years old. As a youth Bingham was apprenticed to a cabinetmaker, who introduced him to a now unknown portrait painter who inspired him to take up the easel. Between 1828 and 1833, he achieved local fame as a portrait painter of uncanny ability. His self-taught photographic style prompted some admirers to send him to Philadelphia to study. In 1833 Bingham exhibited *Western Boatmen Ashore* at the Apollo Gallery in New York. Between 1841 and 1844 his fame grew, and he received commissions to paint the portraits of many well-known politicians of the day, among them, John Quincy Adams. His career truly blossomed, however, with a series of paintings depicting daily life along the Missouri and Mississippi Rivers. When he returned to Missouri in 1845, he became fascinated by the workings of the political life he had so often depicted. In 1848 he was elected to represent Saline County in the State Legislature. He continued to paint political pictures, now from personal experience, and became a prominent fixture in the world of American art. In 1856, Bingham sailed for Europe and studied for two years in Dusseldorf, as had many American artists before him. His style became both more refined and energetic, and his return to the United States marked an even more vigorous period for him in both painting and politics. After the Civil War Bingham became an important figure in the Democratic Party of Missouri, finally serving as Adjutant General in 1875. In 1877 he was appointed a full professor at the Missouri School of Art. He died in Kansas City. Bingham fascinated his contemporaries, who viewed the extraordinary realism of his work with awe. Even today, many critics are at a loss to explain how someone exclusively self-taught early in his career could produce such photographically realistic works; he does not fit into any particular school, and his expertise was remarkable for an artist working in the newly settled Missouri frontier.

Fur Traders Descending the Missouri (1845)
This famed painting would probably have been considered a masterpiece, had it been created in Europe. However, its sense of mood, calm, physical exactitude, and color harmony make it nothing less than a marvel when one considers that it is the work of a self-taught frontier man. The muddiness of the river, the hard-bitten faces of the traders, the mysterious diffidence of the black cat all combine to make this a painting of richness and enduring interest.

SETH EASTMAN

Government patronage of Western artists was realized most successfully in the realistic works of Seth Eastman (1808–1875), who was an officer in the U.S. Army from 1824 until his death. Eastman was born in Brunswick, Maine, and was nominated as a cadet to the U.S. Military Academy when he was sixteen. There, he studied drawing with Thomas Gimbrede, and also studied privately with C.R. Leslie and Robert W. Weir. In 1833 he was appointed assistant drawing instructor at the Academy. His excellent views of the Hudson Valley region were exhibited at the National Academy of Design, to which he was elected an honorary member. Eastman's interest in the West, and in Indians in particular, began in 1840, when he took part in the Seminole War in Florida and sketched the captives. On his return to Fort Snelling, in Minnesota, he began sketching local Indians. But it was when he was transferred to Texas, in 1848, that his career as a painter truly flowered. From that time on, Eastman worked in a governmental capacity. In 1849, as an illustrator for the Office of Indian Affairs, he prepared 300 drawings to illustrate *Indian Tribes of the United States*. He returned to frontier duty in 1856, incorporating painting into his normal military duties. During the Civil War, he attained the rank of Brigadier General and suffered injuries that incapacitated him. So prominent had he become that by 1867—following the war and his recovery—he was commissioned by a joint resolution of Congress to paint pictures for the Capitol building. In 1870, he painted seventeen pictures for the House Committee on Military Affairs. He died in Washington in 1875. Part of Eastman's strength came from his unswerving dedication to realism and his vigorous avoidance of romantic license. His pictures are a faithful chronicle of the events and people Eastman experienced and saw. His technique was more sophisticated than that of Catlin and more true to detail than Miller's. He did not shy from illustrating violence among the Indians, refusing to idealize them as so many others had done. Eastman was a craftsman dedicated to the ideal of a near photographic representation of the world—as it was, rather than as it was desired to be.

Lacrosse Playing Among the Sioux Indians (1852)
This work displays the vitality that infuses many of Eastman's works. He skillfully portrays the action of the often violent game without sacrificing detail or compositional integrity, using bright colors to heighten the excitement of the scene. There is an almost photographic neutrality to this work, a quality that is an essential characteristic of Eastman's entire artistic output.

JOHN MIX STANLEY

John Mix Stanley (1814–1872), like Catlin, had early experiences with Indians that eventually were to turn his life's attention toward the West—his father owned a tavern in Canandaigua, New York, that was frequented by Indians from the nearby reservations. Stanley was orphaned at an early age. After his parents' death, he was apprenticed to a coachmaker. However, unhappy with this, he moved to Detroit, where he worked as a housepainter. There, he made the acquaintance of several wealthy men who underwrote the costs of a trip to Italy for him. His interest in the fine arts was awakened in Italy, and on his return he began formal art training with James Bowman in Philadelphia. Between 1837 and 1839, he made a living as a portraitist. In 1839, he met and painted some Indians at Fort Snelling, Minnesota. Like Catlin, Miller, and Eastman, these encounters with Indians changed his life's orientation. Stanley began travelling along the Mississippi and through the plains states. In 1846, he joined Major Stephen W. Kearney's military expedition to California, during which he saw action against the Mexicans at San Diego. Stanley was thus one of the long line of Western artists associated with the military. In 1851, he followed Catlin's path by creating an Indian Gallery, which was shown successfully in the East. Ultimately, he settled in Washington, D.C., where he was a founding trustee of the National Gallery. He continued to paint successfully until his death in Detroit in 1872. Stanley's ambition to have the government purchase his extensive portfolio of paintings of Indians was never fulfilled. His surviving works—over 200 of his paintings were destroyed by fire during his lifetime—reveal clearly that he was a chronicler and a painter of the exotic as well as the familiar; he spent much effort, for example, detailing the odd flora and fauna of the Gila River in New Mexico. He was one of the last artist-observers who attempted to capture the wild atmosphere of the West before it was tamed by the spreading culture of the East.

The Buffalo Hunt (1855)
Stanley's *Buffalo Hunt* contrasts strongly with Catlin's work on the same subject. Here, the Indians are indeed "surrounding" their prey, and groups of Indians are seen attacking individual buffalo in concert. The technique is detailed and accurate, reflecting his formal academic training, with just a hint of the moody romanticism that was beginning to creep into the works of Stanley's contemporaries. This picture is an engaging rendition of an exciting event that Stanley sketched in the field. It has the immediacy of journalism as well as the color and allure of good storytelling.

ARTHUR FITZWILLIAM (A.F.) TAIT

Among the many Europeans who migrated to America to find their fortune, Arthur Tait (1819–1905) was unique; he was already a success in England when he arrived. Tait was born and raised in Liverpool. His family was poverty stricken, and he left school at fourteen. His interest in the arts led him to seek an apprenticeship in the field, at Agnew's Art Dealers in Manchester. He was, at the time, particularly fascinated by sculpture, and at night he studied casting at the Royal Manchester Institute; it proved to be his only formal training. In 1840 George Catlin brought his magnificent Indian Gallery to London, and in 1841 young Tait was hired by Catlin to help him manage the gallery. As with so many other artists who were to render the American West, Catlin's influence on Tait was tremendous. When Catlin took the Indian Gallery to Paris, in the years 1845 to 1848, Tait accompanied him. In Paris, Tait was quickly convinced that the exotic American West was a subject of great importance, and, being ambitious, he determined to head for America himself. With Catlin's help, he left for New York in 1850. Tait was immediately successful. He opened a studio on Broadway, and built a rural camp for himself at Long Lake in the Adirondacks. In 1852, Nathaniel Currier's new partner, Charles Merritt Ives, met and hired Tait. While the selling price of the average Currier and Ives print ranged from five cents to two dollars, Tait's works often brought three dollars or more per print. Because Tait was an independent artist and not an employee, Currier and Ives used only the finest reproduction techniques and hand coloring for Tait's paintings. Tait never went farther west than Chicago, and, according to Colin Simkin, "[his] researches were done in the Astor Library, on illustrations by Bodmer and Catlin...He was a skilled academic painter in a community which had no acquaintance with the best in art." Yet, Tait's extraordinary sense of drama and his strong renderings thrilled many Americans. His Currier and Ives lithographs proved to be the most popular the firm ever produced. In fact, in 1928, the record price for a Currier and Ives went to Tait's series, *The Life of a Hunter*.

The Life of a Hunter "A Tight Fix" (ca. 1862)
This famed picture is typical of Tait's bold, dramatic style. Pictorial elements are all subordinated to narrative here: the bear is wounded and maddened; the red of the blood stands out from the predominant blacks and whites. The hunter is shown about to stab the animal, emphasizing his mythical bravery in the face of overwhelming odds. Behind a tree to the rear right, another hunter is aiming a rifled musket at the bear: will he kill the bear in time? This work surely held its viewers enthralled. It is, in its small way, a masterpiece of the kind of illustration that was later to transform Western art from anthropology to mythology.

ALBERT BIERSTADT

The monumental works of Albert Bierstadt (1830–1902) drastically changed the nature of Western art. His was the first truly nonanthropological sensibility to undertake the depiction of Western subject matter. His imagination encompassed the vast spaces of the West while his colors and perspectives reflected his mind's reaction to what he saw. Bierstadt was born in Solingen, Germany, and moved with his family to Bedford, Massachusetts when he was two. By the age of twenty, he was teaching art in that town and publishing illustrations in its local newspaper. By 1853, he had exhibited at the Academy of Fine Arts in Boston. A self-taught painter, Bierstadt chafed at his limitations. In 1854, he travelled to Dusseldorf, the center of art study to which so many gravitated in the mid-nineteenth century, and the successor to Munich as the center of Romanticism. After travelling through Europe, he returned to Bedford in 1857. In 1859, tired of the East, he joined an expedition to the Rocky Mountains. This journey changed his life forever. He was overwhelmed by the scale of the landscape, and his first Western paintings, such as *The Oregon Trail* and *The Rocky Mountains*, were vast not only in canvas area—often covering whole walls—but also in the magnificence of their vision. Bierstadt gained an immediate and sensational popularity. Huge crowds gathered to pay a quarter or more apiece to see his paintings on display. Bierstadt's new wealth permitted him to travel extensively. He continued to paint in the same manner until 1889, when, in a sudden reversal, his work began to fall into critical disregard. The Paris Exposition rejected his *The Last of the Buffalo* as "not current," and, in 1893, his *Landing of Columbus* was refused for the Chicago World's Columbian Exposition. From then on, Bierstadt experienced the terrible humiliation of being considered "old fashioned." Bitter and almost bankrupt, he rescued his work *The Rocky Mountains* from destruction by purchasing it himself for $5,000; it had originally sold for $25,000. He died, a broken man, in New York City in 1902. Bierstadt has suffered criticism both from traditionalists who feel he exaggerated nature without justification and from modernists who feel he was insufficiently subjective. The truth lies somewhere in between. His once discounted works are now regaining critical appreciation for their scope, care, and emotional impact. His intense Romanticism marked the beginning of a new era of art in America which was highly personal in content, feeling, and motivation. Bierstadt was the first of the truly nonanthropological, completely Romantic artists of the West.

Buffalo Trail: The Impending Storm (1869)
The subjective, dramatic elements of Bierstadt's art are fully present in this large work. The dark, turbulent sky has a truly melodramatic quality of threat, and the lead buffalo is followed by a long line of animals trying to outpace the following storm. It is obvious, in a narrative sense, that the race is close to being lost; the wildly twisted trees and grass show that the wind is already fierce. A sense of impending doom is mixed with wild excitement in this typically theatrical work, with its exaggerated green foliage and smoky sky. Its impact is immediate and strong, and it is filled with Romantic fervor.

THOMAS MORAN

Unlike the works of Bierstadt, those of Thomas Moran (1837–1925), with their distinctive steer-shaped monogram and thumbprint for verification, have never ceased to be in demand. Moran combined ardent Romanticism with extraordinary draftsmanship. His works, highly idealized and colored, are detailed and refined to a degree unmatched by any other landscapist of the American West. Moran was born in Lancashire, England, but moved with his family to Philadelphia in 1845. He was apprenticed to sketch designs on wood for the firm of Scattergood and Telfer in 1853, but gave that up to devote himself entirely to painting in 1856. Primarily self-taught, he exhibited his first work at the Pennsylvania Academy in 1858. In 1861, after working and studying under his lithographer brother, Edward, he travelled to London, where he studied the works of Turner and Claude Lorrain, and in 1866, he travelled to Paris, where he was greatly influenced by the work of Corot. After nine months in Paris, he went to Venice, where he began to sketch watercolor studies, a technique which later was to be of great value to him. In 1871 Moran made his first trip to the West, with the surveying party of F.V. Hayden. Here he was exposed to the great wonders of Yellowstone, with its hot springs, canyons, and mountains. He determined that these wonders should be preserved in their natural state, and produced a prodigious series of field watercolors and large canvases representing these phenomena in idealized terms. The public reaction was overwhelming. In 1872 Congress declared Yellowstone the nation's first national park, and much of the public credit went to Moran, whose works were purchased by the government. His fame endured for the remainder of his life. He travelled through the West and through Europe extensively, and lived to be a prosperous 90-year-old firebrand who spent a good deal of time railing against "modern art." Unlike Bierstadt, Moran never suffered a critical decline. Obsessed with his work to the end, he spent his last minutes describing scenes that he had yet to paint as he saw them on the ceiling of his bedroom. He died in Santa Barbara, California. It was due to Moran's tremendous impact that the primitivism formerly acceptable in the works of so many Western artists became discredited. Although some critics assailed his idealization of his subject matter, the public was unaffected. Moran remains one of the great masters of Western art.

Great Falls-Grand Canyon of the Yellowstone (1895)
This work epitomizes Moran's vast skill and tremendous subtlety. The vertical composition is enhanced by the delicacy of the lines that delineate both the falls and the surrounding rocks. The subtle coloration of the atmosphere, filled with mist from the crashing water, contrasts with the strong but fine outlines of the massive rock formations that form the river's bed. The work is atmospheric in the extreme. Moran's paintings are unique in that they combine realistic representation with a Romantic sensitivity to the grandeur and infinite variety of nature.

CHARLES MARION RUSSELL

Charles Marion Russell (1864–1926) was the only true cowboy among the great artists of the American West. His fellow cowhands considered him a mediocre cowboy but an excellent artist. In any case, he had a unique perspective on his subject matter, and the technique to present it with telling impact. Russell was born in Missouri, and was fascinated by the West throughout his childhood. He failed in one school after another, and in an effort to break his Western fantasies, his father sent him to work on a sheep ranch in Montana. He never went back to school; from 1880 to 1892, he worked on ranches and in cattle drives. Russell began his artistic career with small clay models he made on the Montana sheep ranch. Following this, in 1885, he began his first serious oils. In 1887, he declined an offer to study art in Philadelphia, and the next year, *Harper's* published one of his works. After travels through the Canadian West, he published *Studies of Western Life,* and its success convinced him to give up the saddle for the brush. Over the next decade he painted and sold illustrations to magazines and newspapers. Then, in 1903, he went to New York, where he sold some of his paintings and, as a result, started to acquire a national reputation. He began to receive government commissions, and in 1914, he took his works to London and Paris, where he was greeted with great acclaim. By the end of his life, he was travelling freely between his homes in California, Montana, and New York City. In 1925, the University of Montana gave him an honorary Doctorate of Law. Russell was one of the most modest and easygoing artists of the Western tradition. Nevertheless, like Bingham, his self-taught technique was formidable. His range of mood was extraordinary, reaching from such impressionistic works as *Lewis and Clark on the Lower Columbia* and the epic *Lewis and Clark Meeting the Flathead Indians at Ross' Hole* to such picturesque works as *The Hold Up*. Russell was almost entirely a narrative painter, for few of his works were simply renditions of a static observation. Unlike Schreyvogel, however, he did not concentrate on the violent aspects of his subject. Even the rollicking *Without Knocking*, picturing a bunch of cowhands barging into a saloon on horseback, has a sense of fun about it; indeed, all his works have a warmth and accessibility that have given them a continuing popularity through the years. Where the works of Remington tended to become philosophical, and those of Schreyvogel were theatrical, those of Russell have the character of storytelling by a campfire.

The Hold Up (1899)
Russell painted this picture after hearing the tale of this holdup related by one of the passengers and then seeing the captured robber hung. The sense of humor in the painting is obvious if one looks at the passengers. They are a motley group, to say the least. The thief is not particularly tense: according to accounts, he knew some of the passengers and conversed with them during the event. No one was injured. This is a work approaching illustration, and like many of Russell's lighter pieces, there is a whimsical quality that is contrasted with the lyrical scenery.

HENRY F. FARNY

Henry F. Farny (1847–1916), one of the key mythologizers of the "Old West," mourned the passing of the Indian, and painted numerous works eulogizing the nomadic civilizations that had been washed away by the flood of white settlement. A painter of impressive imagination, his paintings often harken back to things, people, and events of which he had no personal knowledge. Farny's father was an official of the French government between 1840 and 1847. When revolution broke out in France, he fled from Alsace with his family and emigrated to America. Young Henry grew up in the woods of Pennsylvania. It was on the local reservation of the Seneca Indians that he first heard and became enchanted by Indian lore. In 1859 his family moved to Cincinnati, a city with which he was to have a lifelong association. In the early 1860s he apprenticed himself to a lithographer, from whom he received his first education in the arts. His progress was rapid. In 1865, *Harper's Weekly* published a two-page spread of his views of Cincinnati. *Harper's* was so excited by his work that they asked him to come East in 1867, and he worked and studied in New York for the better part of a year before embarking by schooner for Italy, where he studied with Thomas Read. Later, Farny made his way to Dusseldorf, at that time a center for American artists abroad. During most of the 1870s, Farny supported himself by producing illustrations for *Harper's* and for Cincinnati newspapers. In 1878 he took a 1000-mile canoe trip down the Missouri River and fell in love with the Far West. By 1881, he had determined to paint portraits of Indians, and produced a memorable portrait of Sitting Bull and a major work recording the forbidden "ghost dance" of the Sioux Nation. He continued painting Indians until his death in 1916, and achieved both critical acclaim and widespread popularity. Farny's views were rarely those of the declining Indian restricted to his reservation and languishing in poverty; his Indians roamed free, their existence unaffected by contact with white settlers. Occasionally Farny relented and composed a work showing the contrast between the Indians' world and the settlers' technology, but even in these he was reluctant to portray Indians as exhausted and enslaved. His work is myth at its most compelling and compassionate.

Song of the Talking Wire (1904)
This famous painting is one of Farny's least mythic works; it accurately portrays the reality of the Indians' sad situation in the early twentieth century. The Indian hunter leans against a telegraph pole, listening to the chatter of the humming wires without understanding. Farny makes us understand how dismayed the Indian must feel in the face of these strange mechanisms that bound together people so far from each other. The work at once symbolizes the appealing naturalness of the Indian and the sadness of his being "outdistanced" by the works of the white man. In its grey colors and in its portrayal of the isolation of the Indian figure, the work is a moving illustration of Farny's protest against the passing of the Indian way of life.

CHARLES SCHREYVOGEL

Charles Schreyvogel (1861–1912), who, along with Remington and Russell formed the trinity of turn-of-the-century Western masters, was born in deep poverty on New York's Lower East Side. He sold newspapers, worked in an office, and went to public schools, unlike the more aristocratic Remington. In his youth his parents moved to Hoboken, and there he became, in turn, a gold engraver, a die sinker, and finally, in 1877, a lithographer. He excelled at this, and became a lithographic artist and a teacher of lithography in 1880. In 1887, patrons sent him to study in Dusseldorf. He returned to New York two years later and attempted a career as a portraitist and landscape artist, at which he failed miserably. In 1893, a chance commission changed his fortune: he was hired to sketch the Buffalo Bill Show. With the money he earned from this, he spent five months on the Colorado Ute Reserve, sketching cowboys, Indians, and soldiers. From there he moved to Arizona, where he sketched cowboys and collected western gear. Schreyvogel returned to New York in 1896 and attempted to continue his career as a lithographer, but his Western works did not sell. Impoverished, he submitted a painting to the National Academy Exhibition. But he left no address or signature, and when the painting, *My Bunkie*, was awarded the $300 first prize, no one knew the artist's name or address. When it was finally discovered that he was the work's author, Schreyvogel became an overnight success. Now financially comfortable, he went West and sketched army troops and Indians in the Dakotas. In 1903, one of his works dealing with Custer was criticized by Remington as "half-baked." A torrent of letters from soldiers who had been present at the scene represented in the painting supported Schreyvogel, and Remington was forced to back down, but the controversy made Schreyvogel a national figure in the arts. Schreyvogel's total output was small—less than 100 oils— but his works were extensively reproduced. He worked out of a studio in Hoboken for the remainder of his brief career, until his death from blood poisoning at the age of fifty-one. An artist of action, there was little of the contemplative about Schreyvogel's highly narrative work. His skill as a draftsman and his dramatic color sense combined with his theatrical subject matter to produce vivid and memorable works. His cowboys are ever in motion, his Indians relentlessly on the attack, his soldiers never at rest. Although he was not really an illustrator, his works convey an epic sense that still inspires viewers today.

The Silenced War Hoop (1903)
This dramatic painting is typical of the works of Schreyvogel: a violent narrative rendered with bold patterns and extremely precise draftsmanship. Here, the leading member of the Indian column has been shot by the trooper, who now withholds his gun as a gesture toward the already dying warrior. The sense of drama is increased by the animation in the horses and men, and is brought to sharp focus by the triangular composition centered on the nose of the dying warrior's fleeing horse.

NEWELL CONVERS WYETH

N.C. Wyeth (1882–1945), the founder of an American art dynasty including his son, Andrew, and grandson, Jamie, was an artist whose Western works were only a part of his enormous output of illustrations. Yet, perhaps no other illustrator has painted the West with such a theatrical art, and no previous artist illustrated so well the myths that produced our notions of the drama of cowboys, Indians, and holdup men. Wyeth was Boston bred and trained, attending Mechanics Art High School, the Massachusetts Normal Art School, and Eric Pape's Art School. After studying with C.W. Reed in Boston, he joined the "Pyle School" of illustrators at Chadds Ford, Pennsylvania. Wyeth venerated Pyle and emulated his approach to art as closely as he was able, painting much the same kind of subject matter. In his immensely long career, Wyeth completed a staggering 3,000-plus works, including over 25 books for Scribner's "Juvenile Classics," many of which are still in print. In addition to his illustrations, Wyeth did both still lifes and tempera landscapes. In his youth, Wyeth travelled extensively in the Southwest. He later returned to the East with a great many sketches which were to form the basis for his almost endless illustrations of life in that region. His first published illustration, *Bucking Bronco*, was for the *Saturday Evening Post* in 1903. Later in his career, he made two more trips to the West, in 1904 for *Scribner's* and in 1906 for *Outing*. After these trips, he never returned to the West again. Wyeth's pictures decorate the most incredible variety of places: hotels, banks, insurance companies, schools, and churches. He was a man of broad education and was particularly fond of historical subjects. His work was aimed at making a fast and lasting impression on the viewer, who was likely to turn the page as fast as he could in order to follow the story being illustrated. For that reason, when considered as art, Wyeth's illustrations have a very melodramatic quality. Nevertheless, he was an excellent draftsman and had a keen feeling for color and composition. His paintings transferred the complex mythologies of Farny and Johnson into easily recognizable symbols that have become part of the vocabulary of art that we now identify as "The Wild West." It is a world far removed from the realities once so painstakingly summarized, chronicled, and recorded by such pioneers as Catlin, such visionaries as Bierstadt, and such luminaries as Remington and Russell. He represents, in some respects, the end of a great era in American art.

Blue Lock, The Queen (1916)
This work was an illustration for a story of the same name that was published in *Collier's Weekly Magazine* of October 21, 1916. In this scene, the mare is being stolen by a renegade Indian, as its owner hurriedly reaches for his carbine. After a climactic battle, the horse is regained by its owner. This illustration has the full quality of Wyeth's best work: a strong narrative sense, fine use of subtle coloration and detail, and expert composition. It is illustration at its best—quickly capturing the viewer's interest and yet entirely memorable.

FRANK TENNEY JOHNSON

Frank Tenney Johnson (1874–1939), like his contemporary Wyeth, was a man who had been passed by history—by the time of his maturity, the great Wild West was gone. But, unlike Wyeth, his youth had been spent watching the great events that wound the Indian Wars to their halt. His mythologies have a deep personal meaning, an epic sense, and a degree of intensity unusual among his contemporaries. Johnson was born on a ranch near Council Bluffs, Iowa, and was educated in the little town of Oconomowoc, Wisconsin. From the age of fourteen, his life was dotted with romantic episodes. At that age he ran away from home and apprenticed himself to the panoramic painter F.W. Heinie in Milwaukee. Then, at fifteen, he studied with former Texas Ranger Richard Lorenz. At the close of the century, Johnson began working as a staff illustrator doing portraits for a Milwaukee newspaper. Then, suddenly restless, he packed up and left for New York in 1902. There he studied at the Art Students League with several noted artists, among them the American Impressionist Henri, who felt that Johnson had a strong talent. During this period he supported himself as a fashion illustrator and newspaper artist. Then, again restless, he spent the summer of 1904 at a ranch in Colorado, sketching cowboys. On his return to New York, the fortuitous event of his life occurred: he met Zane Grey and was contracted to illustrate his novels. For fifteen years Johnson did so, and in the process became a national figure. In 1920 Johnson followed Clyde Forsythe to Alhambra, California, where they established a studio that hosted some of the West's leading artists: Russell, Edward Borein, and also Norman Rockwell and Dean Cornwell. During that time, Johnson perfected his technique for painting nocturnal scenes, works on which a good part of his fame still rests. He flourished as both an artist and an illustrator for another nineteen years. Finally, in 1939, he died in Los Angeles of spinal meningitis. Johnson's works for Zane Grey developed much of the visual mythology that was to appear in both the silent and sound films about the West. His views of cowboys from ground level tended to make them larger than life, with grim expressions that convey a feeling of silent determination. There is an even deeper sense of tragedy in his portrayals of Indians. A contemplative artist, the emotions of his pictures are always subordinate to a philosophical or conceptual tension in his work, in which things are clearly about to happen, but nothing has been resolved.

Riders of the Dawn (ca. 1925)
The title of this popular work is remarkably close to that of one of the Zane Grey novels he illustrated: Riders of the Purple Sage. The painting is non-narrative: the cowboys are probably riding the range looking for strays, but their motivation is not really clear. They are seen approaching, and from slightly below, so that they tend to have an impending impact on the viewer, which gives them a relentless quality. The Impressionistic treatment of the background transforms this work into a mood piece of subtle and multifaceted content.